10-06

# A Heart for Jesus

## by Juanita Bynum

### Illustrated by Cathy Ann Johnson

Charisma
KIDS

A STRANG COMPANY

A Heart for Jesus
by Juanita Bynum

Requests for information may be addressed to:

The children's book imprint of Strang Communications Company
600 Rinehart Rd., Lake Mary, FL 32746
www.charismakids.com

Children's Editor: Gwen Ellis
Copyeditor: Jevon Oakman Bolden
Design Director: Mark Poulalion
Designed by Joe De Leon, Ederón Hernández, and Tatia Lockridge

Library of Congress Control Number 2004101621
International Standard Book Number 1-59185-206-4

05 06 07 08 09 — 98765432
Printed in China

This book is presented to:

_____

From:

_____

Date:

_____

On Sunday, Mom said she gave her heart to Jesus.
I'm not sure what that means.

I heard her heart beating when
she gave me a hug just then.

On Monday, Mom smiled
and made me
oatmeal for breakfast.

When I spilled the milk,
I felt so bad. Mom didn't even
get upset. She said it was OK.
She cleaned up the milk and
poured me a new glass.

She gave me a hug, and
I could hear her heart beating.

I heard it again when she read me a story.

She picked me up and kissed my knee when I fell.
And there was that heart beating...

...thumpa thump thump.

I could hear it **thumpa thump** when she rocked me to sleep.

"Mom,
you still have a heart.
Did you really
give it to Jesus?"

"Yes, child. But I didn't give Him the heart that beats
in my chest. I gave Jesus my feelings, my thoughts,
my ideas, and my wishes.

"Now, when I feel sad or afraid, Jesus understands and makes me feel better. When I get tired of being kind to others, I ask Jesus to give me strength. When there is something very special that I want or need, I can ask Jesus for it.

He never runs out of joy...

courage...

patience...

or strength"

"Sometimes I feel sad inside. Sometimes I feel afraid.
I want to have a new heart from Jesus, too!"

"You can.
All you have to do is ask."

"Tell us, how do we give
our hearts to Jesus?"

"You don't give the heart that beats in your body to Jesus.

"You give Him your feelings...He feels with you.
You give Him your thoughts...He thinks with you.
You give Him your ideas and wishes...

He helps you make those wishes come true."

"How do I give Jesus all those things?"

"Yeah, I can't see them or touch them."

"Just talk to Jesus in prayer
He can hear you wherever you are.
He cares about your feelings…
your thoughts…
your wishes…

"Jesus wants to be part of your life.
When you tell Him about the things
that worry you
and ask for His help,
it is like giving those things
to Him to take care of."

Jesus, I believe You love me.
The Bible says You love me
so much that You died to
take away my sins. Please
forgive me for the wrong
things that I have done.

Make my heart clean and new.
Fill me with Your love and joy
and courage. Be with me every day.
Help me live and love others the
way You do. I ask in Your name.
Amen.

Dear Parents,

Many of the concepts about Christianity are very hard for children, with their concrete thinking, to understand. One of those hard-to-understand concepts is the idea of "giving your heart to Jesus." Just how do you explain what it means to give your heart to Jesus?

Juanita Bynum has done a great job of explaining the process. She says that it is not the heart that beats in our chests that we give to Jesus, but it is our feelings, our thoughts, our worries, and our wishes.

In exchange Jesus gives us strength to be kind to others. He gives us joy and courage and patience, too. He gives us a hope and future. And *He* gives us the opportunity to ask for what we need.

Juanita Bynum also explains in simple language that to give our hearts to Jesus, all we have to do it talk to *Him* in prayer. Great comfort comes to a child when he understands that Jesus loves him, lives with him, and will never leave him.

Many children come to understand about salvation earlier than parents might expect. Bynum has included a simple prayer for children to pray, asking Jesus to make their hearts new and clean. If your child expresses an interest in "giving his heart to Jesus," by all means, take it seriously and pray either the prayer given in the book with him or another you make up.

Leading your child to accept Jesus as his Savior is one of the greatest experiences a child can have.